Journal

And he said unto me, Write.
REVELATION 21:5

BARBOUR
PUBLISHING

ISBN 978-1-59789-436-4 (Daisy—Photo © Digital Vision)
ISBN 978-1-59789-437-1 (Pink)
ISBN 978-1-59789-438-8 (Dandelion—Image © iStock Photo)
ISBN 978-1-59789-439-5 (Stripes—Photo © iStock Photo)

All scripture quotations are taken from the King James Version
of the Bible.

Published by Barbour Publishing, Inc., P.O. Box 719,
Uhrichsville, Ohio 44683 www.barbourbooks.com

*Our mission is to publish and distribute inspirational products
offering exceptional value and biblical encouragement to the masses.*

Member of the
Evangelical Christian
Publishers Association

Printed in Thailand.
5 4 3 2

Every word of God is pure: he is a shield unto them
that put their trust in him.
PROVERBS 30:5

_____

_____

_____

_____

_____

_____

_____

_____

_____

_____

_____

_____

_____

Behold, God is my salvation; I will trust, and not be afraid: for the LORD JEHOVAH is my strength and my song.
ISAIAH 12:2

*God is love; and he that dwelleth in love dwelleth in God,
and God in him.*
1 JOHN 4:16

_____

_____

_____

_____

_____

_____

_____

_____

_____

_____

_____

_____

_____

_____

_But the LORD is my defence; and my God
is the rock of my refuge._
PSALM 94:22

Thou art worthy, O Lord, to receive glory and honour and power: for thou hast created all things, and for thy pleasure they are and were created.

REVELATION 4:11

_____

_____

_____

_____

_____

_____

_____

_____

_____

_____

_____

_____

_____

_____

_____

_____

Behold, what manner of love the Father hath bestowed upon us, that we should be called the sons of God.
1 JOHN 3:1

The earth is full of the goodness of the LORD.
PSALM 33:5

_____

_____

_____

_____

_____

_____

_____

_____

_____

_____

_____

_____

_____

_____

_____

I am come that they might have life, and that they might have it more abundantly.

JOHN 10:10

To the Lord our God belong mercies and forgivenesses.
DANIEL 9:9

_____

_____

_____

_____

_____

_____

_____

_____

_____

_____

_____

_____

_____

_____

_____

_____

I will be glad and rejoice in thee: I will sing praise to thy name, O thou most High.
PSALM 9:2

*The fruit of the Spirit is love, joy, peace, longsuffering,
gentleness, goodness, faith, meekness, temperance:
against such there is no law.*
GALATIANS 5:22–23

_____

_____

_____

_____

_____

_____

_____

_____

_____

_____

_____

_____

_____

_____

_____

The LORD is good, a strong hold in the day of trouble; and he knoweth them that trust in him.
NAHUM 1:7

Be glad in the LORD, and rejoice, ye righteous: and shout for joy,
all ye that are upright in heart.

PSALM 32:11

_____

_____

_____

_____

_____

_____

_____

_____

_____

_____

_____

_____

_____

_____

Whoso keepeth his word, in him verily is the love of God perfected: hereby know we that we are in him.
1 JOHN 2:5

*Light is sown for the righteous, and gladness for
the upright in heart.*
PSALM 97:11

_____

_____

_____

_____

_____

_____

_____

_____

_____

_____

_____

_____

_____

The blessing of the LORD, it maketh rich,
and he addeth no sorrow with it.
PROVERBS 10:22

And this is the promise that he hath promised us,
even eternal life.
1 JOHN 2:25

_____

_____

_____

_____

_____

_____

_____

_____

_____

_____

_____

_____

_____

_____

_____

_____

I will rejoice in the LORD, I will joy in the God of my salvation.
HABAKKUK 3:18

Let us not be weary in well doing: for in due season
we shall reap, if we faint not.
GALATIANS 6:9

_____

_____

_____

_____

_____

_____

_____

_____

_____

_____

_____

_____

_____

_____

Blessed be the God and Father of our Lord Jesus Christ,
who hath blessed us with all spiritual blessings in
heavenly places in Christ.
EPHESIANS 1:3

Now then we are ambassadors for Christ.
2 CORINTHIANS 5:20

_____

_____

_____

_____

_____

_____

_____

_____

_____

_____

_____

_____

_____

_____

_____

_____

For his anger endureth but a moment; in his favour is life: weeping may endure for a night, but joy cometh in the morning.

PSALM 30:5

Seek ye first the kingdom of God, and his righteousness;
and all these things shall be added unto you.
MATTHEW 6:33

_____

_____

_____

_____

_____

_____

_____

_____

_____

_____

_____

_____

_____

Thou art my hiding place and my shield: I hope in thy word.
PSALM 119:114

And he saith unto me, Write, Blessed are they which are called unto the marriage supper of the Lamb.
REVELATION 19:9

_____
_____
_____
_____
_____
_____
_____
_____
_____
_____
_____
_____
_____
_____
_____
_____
_____
_____

_Thou, O Lord, art a God full of compassion, and gracious,
long suffering, and plenteous in mercy and truth._
PSALM 86:15

*Blessed are the peacemakers: for they shall be called
the children of God.*
MATTHEW 5:9

_____

_____

_____

_____

_____

_____

_____

_____

_____

_____

_____

_____

_____

_____

_____

_____

_Blessed is he whose transgression is forgiven,
whose sin is covered._
PSALM 32:1

Prove all things; hold fast that which is good.
1 THESSALONIANS 5:21

_____

_____

_____

_____

_____

_____

_____

_____

_____

_____

_____

_____

I sought the LORD, and he heard me, and delivered me from all my fears.
PSALM 34:4

I am come a light into the world, that whosoever believeth on me should not abide in darkness.

JOHN 12:46

_____

_____

_____

_____

_____

_____

_____

_____

_____

_____

_____

_____

_____

_____

_____

_____

Let brotherly love continue.
HEBREWS 13:1

Blessed are the pure in heart: for they shall see God.
MATTHEW 5:8

_____

_____

_____

_____

_____

_____

_____

_____

_____

_____

_____

_____

_____

_____

_____

_____

And my soul shall be joyful in the LORD:
it shall rejoice in his salvation.
PSALM 35:9

Be not overcome of evil, but overcome evil with good.
ROMANS 12:21

_____

_____

_____

_____

_____

_____

_____

_____

_____

_____

_____

_____

_____

_____

_____

_____

Some trust in chariots, and some in horses: but we will
remember the name of the LORD our God.
PSALM 20:7

And all flesh shall see the salvation of God.
LUKE 3:6

_____

_____

_____

_____

_____

_____

_____

_____

_____

_____

_____

_____

_____

_____

_____

_____

Serve the LORD with gladness: come before his presence with singing.
PSALM 100:2

*The LORD liveth; and blessed be my rock; and exalted
be the God of the rock of my salvation.*
2 SAMUEL 22:47

_____

_____

_____

_____

_____

_____

_____

_____

_____

_____

_____

_____

_____

And because ye are sons, God hath sent forth the Spirit of his Son into your hearts, crying, Abba, Father.
GALATIANS 4:6

Giving thanks unto the Father, which hath made us meet to be partakers of the inheritance of the saints in light.
COLOSSIANS 1:12

_____

_____

_____

_____

_____

_____

_____

_____

_____

_____

_____

_____

_____

_____

Let the saints be joyful in glory: let them sing aloud upon their beds.
PSALM 149:5

*The peace of God, which passeth all understanding, shall keep
your hearts and minds through Christ Jesus.*
PHILIPPIANS 4:7

_____

_____

_____

_____

_____

_____

_____

_____

_____

_____

_____

_____

_____

_____

_____

_____

_____

Gracious is the LORD, and righteous; yea, our God is merciful.
PSALM 116:5

By faith ye stand.
2 CORINTHIANS 1:24

_____

_____

_____

_____

_____

_____

_____

_____

_____

_____

_____

_____

_____

_____

_____

_____

Reckon ye also yourselves to be dead indeed unto sin, but alive unto God through Jesus Christ our Lord.
ROMANS 6:11

Be thou my strong habitation, whereunto I may continually resort: thou hast given commandment to save me; for thou art my rock and my fortress.

PSALM 71:3

_____

_____

_____

_____

_____

_____

_____

_____

_____

_____

_____

_____

_____

_____

_____

_____

_____

Greater is he that is in you, than he that is in the world.
1 John 4:4

It is of the LORD's mercies that we are not consumed, because his compassions fail not. They are new every morning: great is thy faithfulness.
LAMENTATIONS 3:22–23

_____

_____

_____

_____

_____

_____

_____

_____

_____

_____

_____

_____

_____

_____

_____

_____

_____

_____

_____

_____

_____

_____

_____

_____

_____

_____

_____

_____

_____

_____

_____

_____

_____

Be kindly affectioned one to another with brotherly love; in honour preferring one another.
ROMANS 12:10

Yea, happy is that people, whose God is the LORD.
PSALM 144:15

_____

_____

_____

_____

_____

_____

_____

_____

_____

_____

_____

_____

_____

_____

_____

_If ye then be risen with Christ, seek those things which are
above, where Christ sitteth on the right hand of God._
COLOSSIANS 3:1

O love the LORD, all ye his saints:
for the LORD preserveth the faithful.
PSALM 31:23

_____

_____

_____

_____

_____

_____

_____

_____

_____

_____

_____

_____

_____

_____

_____

_____

My help cometh from the LORD, which made heaven and earth.
PSALM 121:2

We glory in tribulations also: knowing that tribulation worketh patience; and patience, experience; and experience, hope.

ROMANS 5:3–4

_____

_____

_____

_____

_____

_____

_____

_____

_____

_____

_____

_____

_____

_____

Make a joyful noise unto God, all ye lands.
PSALM 66:1

Ask, and it shall be given you; seek, and ye shall find;
knock, and it shall be opened unto you.
MATTHEW 7:7

_____

_____

_____

_____

_____

_____

_____

_____

_____

_____

_____

_____

_____

_____

_____

_____

_____

_____

Owe no man any thing, but to love one another: for he that loveth another hath fulfilled the law.
ROMANS 13:8

The LORD is my rock, and my fortress, and my deliverer;
my God, my strength, in whom I will trust; my buckler,
and the horn of my salvation, and my high tower.
PSALM 18:2

_____

_____

_____

_____

_____

_____

_____

_____

_____

_____

_____

_____

_____

_____

_____

_____

Blessed are the meek: for they shall inherit the earth.
MATTHEW 5:5

Blessed is the people that know the joyful sound: they shall walk,
O LORD, in the light of thy countenance.
PSALM 89:15

_____

_____

_____

_____

_____

_____

_____

_____

_____

_____

_____

_____

_____

_____

_____

_____

_____

_____

_____

_____

_____

_____

_____

_____

_____

_____

_____

_____

_____

_____

_____

_____

_____

_____

Mercy unto you, and peace, and love, be multiplied.
JUDE 2

For the LORD God is a sun and shield: the LORD will give grace and glory: no good thing will he withhold from them that walk uprightly.

PSALM 84:11

_____

_____

_____

_____

_____

_____

_____

_____

_____

_____

_____

_____

_____

_____

_____

_____

_____

The kingdom of God is not meat and drink; but righteousness, and peace, and joy in the Holy Ghost.
ROMANS 14:17

*And the ransomed of the LORD shall return, and come to Zion
with songs and everlasting joy upon their heads: they shall
obtain joy and gladness, and sorrow and sighing shall flee away.*

ISAIAH 35:10

_____

_____

_____

_____

_____

_____

_____

_____

_____

_____

_____

_____

_____

_____

_____

In thee, O Lord, do I hope: thou wilt hear, O Lord my God.
PSALM 38:15

Let your moderation be known unto all men.
The Lord is at hand.
PHILIPPIANS 4:5

_____

_____

_____

_____

_____

_____

_____

_____

_____

_____

_____

_____

_____

_____

The joy of the LORD is your strength.
NEHEMIAH 8:10

For the scripture saith, Whosoever believeth on him
shall not be ashamed.
ROMANS 10:11

_____

_____

_____

_____

_____

_____

_____

_____

_____

_____

_____

_____

_____

_____

_____

Have not I commanded thee? Be strong and of a good courage; be not afraid, neither be thou dismayed: for the LORD thy God is with thee whithersoever thou goest.
JOSHUA 1:9

Blessed are they that mourn: for they shall be comforted.
MATTHEW 5:4

_____

_____

_____

_____

_____

_____

_____

_____

_____

_____

_____

_____

_____

_____

_____

Sing aloud unto God our strength: make a joyful noise unto the God of Jacob.
PSALM 81:1

He that believeth on the Son hath everlasting life.
JOHN 3:36

_____

_____

_____

_____

_____

_____

_____

_____

_____

_____

_____

_____

_____

_____

_____

_____

And now, Lord, what wait I for? my hope is in thee.
PSALM 39:7

*Every good gift and every perfect gift is from above, and
cometh down from the Father of lights, with whom is no
variableness, neither shadow of turning.*
JAMES 1:17

_____

_____

_____

_____

_____

_____

_____

_____

_____

_____

_____

_____

_____

_____

For the LORD is good; his mercy is everlasting; and his truth endureth to all generations.
PSALM 100:5

*Hope maketh not ashamed; because the love of God is shed
abroad in our hearts by the Holy Ghost which is given unto us.*
ROMANS 5:5

_____

_____

_____

_____

_____

_____

_____

_____

_____

_____

_____

_____

_____

_____

_____

_____

_____

Make a joyful noise unto the LORD, all ye lands.
PSALM 100:1

*Eye hath not seen, nor ear heard, neither have entered
into the heart of man, the things which God
hath prepared for them that love him.*

1 CORINTHIANS 2:9

_____

_____

_____

_____

_____

_____

_____

_____

_____

_____

_____

_____

_____

_____

_____

_____

_____

_____

_____

Sing, O heavens; and be joyful, O earth; and break forth into singing, O mountains: for the LORD hath comforted his people, and will have mercy upon his afflicted.

ISAIAH 49:13

I am the living bread which came down from heaven:
if any man eat of this bread, he shall live for ever.
JOHN 6:51

_____

_____

_____

_____

_____

_____

_____

_____

_____

_____

_____

_____

_____

_____

_____

_____

_____

Let your light so shine before men, that they may see your good works, and glorify your Father which is in heaven.
MATTHEW 5:16

Oh that men would praise the LORD for his goodness,
and for his wonderful works to the children of men!
PSALM 107:8

_____

_____

_____

_____

_____

_____

_____

_____

_____

_____

_____

_____

_____

_____

I am the good shepherd: the good shepherd giveth
his life for the sheep.
JOHN 10:11

O my God, I trust in thee: let me not be ashamed,
let not mine enemies triumph over me.
PSALM 25:2

_____

_____

_____

_____

_____

_____

_____

_____

_____

_____

_____

_____

_____

_____

_____

_____

_____

_____

Let us therefore come boldly unto the throne of grace, that we may obtain mercy, and find grace to help in time of need.
HEBREWS 4:16

Because thou hast been my help, therefore in the shadow
of thy wings will I rejoice.
PSALM 63:7

_____
_____
_____
_____
_____
_____
_____
_____
_____
_____
_____
_____
_____
_____
_____

Is any among you afflicted? let him pray. Is any merry?
let him sing psalms.
JAMES 5:13

Ask, and ye shall receive, that your joy may be full.
JOHN 16:24

_____

_____

_____

_____

_____

_____

_____

_____

_____

_____

_____

_____

_____

_____

Not unto us, O LORD, not unto us, but unto thy name give glory, for thy mercy, and for thy truth's sake.
PSALM 115:1

I will greatly rejoice in the LORD, my soul shall be joyful in my God; for he hath clothed me with the garments of salvation.

ISAIAH 61:10

_____

_____

_____

_____

_____

_____

_____

_____

_____

_____

_____

_____

_____

_____

_____

Behold, the eye of the LORD is upon them that fear him, upon them that hope in his mercy.
PSALM 33:18

Let the peace of God rule in your hearts.
COLOSSIANS 3:15

_____

_____

_____

_____

_____

_____

_____

_____

_____

_____

_____

_____

_____

Now the God of hope fill you with all joy and peace in believing, that ye may abound in hope, through the power of the Holy Ghost.
ROMANS 15:13

I will both lay me down in peace, and sleep: for thou, LORD, only makest me dwell in safety.
PSALM 4:8

_____

_____

_____

_____

_____

_____

_____

_____

_____

_____

_____

_____

_____

_____

_____

He satisfieth the longing soul, and filleth the hungry soul with goodness.
PSALM 107:9

There is none holy as the LORD: for there is none beside thee: neither is there any rock like our God.

1 SAMUEL 2:2

_____

_____

_____

_____

_____

_____

_____

_____

_____

_____

_____

_____

_____

_____

_____

The righteous shall be glad in the LORD, and shall trust in him; and all the upright in heart shall glory.
PSALM 64:10

*Now faith is the substance of things hoped for,
the evidence of things not seen.*
HEBREWS 11:1

_____

_____

_____

_____

_____

_____

_____

_____

_____

_____

_____

_____

_____

_____

_____

_____

_____

_____

_____

_____

_____

_____

_____

_____

_____

_____

_____

_____

_____

_____

_____

_____

_____

I will sing unto the LORD, because he hath dealt bountifully with me.
PSALM 13:6

Jesus said unto her, I am the resurrection, and the life: he that
believeth in me, though he were dead, yet shall he live.
JOHN 11:25

_____

_____

_____

_____

_____

_____

_____

_____

_____

_____

_____

_____

_____

_____

_____

Trust in the LORD, and do good; so shalt thou dwell in the land, and verily thou shalt be fed.

PSALM 37:3

Blessed is the man that endureth temptation: for when he is tried, he shall receive the crown of life, which the Lord hath promised to them that love him.

JAMES 1:12

_____

_____

_____

_____

_____

_____

_____

_____

_____

_____

_____

_____

_____

_____

_____

Trust in the LORD with all thine heart; and lean not unto thine own understanding.
PROVERBS 3:5

As the hart panteth after the water brooks,
so panteth my soul after thee, O God.
PSALM 42:1

_____

_____

_____

_____

_____

_____

_____

_____

_____

_____

_____

_____

_____

_____

_____

_____

_____

Thy faith hath saved thee; go in peace.
LUKE 7:50

And be ye kind one to another, tenderhearted, forgiving one another, even as God for Christ's sake hath forgiven you.
EPHESIANS 4:32

_____

_____

_____

_____

_____

_____

_____

_____

_____

_____

_____

_____

_____

_____

But as many as received him, to them gave he power to become the sons of God, even to them that believe on his name.
JOHN 1:12

Surely goodness and mercy shall follow me all the days of my
life: and I will dwell in the house of the LORD for ever.

PSALM 23:6

_____

_____

_____

_____

_____

_____

_____

_____

_____

_____

_____

_____

_____

_____

There is joy in the presence of the angels of God over one sinner that repenteth.
LUKE 15:10

*And we know that all things work together for good
to them that love God, to them who are the called
according to his purpose.*
ROMANS 8:28

If we love one another, God dwelleth in us, and his love is perfected in us.
1 JOHN 4:12

Blessed be the Lord, who daily loadeth us with benefits,
even the God of our salvation.
PSALM 68:19

_____

_____

_____

_____

_____

_____

_____

_____

_____

_____

_____

_____

_____

_____

_____

_____

_____

Let patience have her perfect work, that ye may be perfect and entire, wanting nothing.
JAMES 1:4

But I will sing of thy power; yea, I will sing aloud of thy mercy
in the morning: for thou hast been my defence
and refuge in the day of my trouble.

PSALM 59:16

_____

_____

_____

_____

_____

_____

_____

_____

_____

_____

_____

_____

_____

_____

_____

_Take good heed therefore unto yourselves,
that ye love the LORD your God._
JOSHUA 23:11

*Beloved, let us love one another: for love is of God; and every
one that loveth is born of God, and knoweth God.*

1 JOHN 4:7

_____

_____

_____

_____

_____

_____

_____

_____

_____

_____

_____

_____

_____

_____

_____

_____

_____

_____

_____

_____

_____

_____

_____

_____

_____

_____

_____

_____

_____

_____

_____

_____

_____

*Be of good courage, and he shall strengthen your heart, all ye
that hope in the LORD.*
PSALM 31:24

Keep yourselves in the love of God, looking for the mercy of our Lord Jesus Christ unto eternal life.

JUDE 21

_____

_____

_____

_____

_____

_____

_____

_____

_____

_____

_____

_____

_____

_____

_____

_____

_____

I love thy commandments above gold; yea, above fine gold.
PSALM 119:127

*The LORD is good unto them that wait for him,
to the soul that seeketh him.*
LAMENTATIONS 3:25

_____

_____
_____
_____

_____
_____
_____

_____
_____
_____

_____
_____
_____

_____
_____
_____

_____
_____
_____

_____
_____
_____

_____
_____
_____

_____

In thy presence is fulness of joy; at thy right hand there are pleasures for evermore.
PSALM 16:11

Thou shalt love the Lord thy God with all thy heart, and with all thy soul, and with all thy mind, and with all thy strength: this is the first commandment.

MARK 12:30

_____

_____

_____

_____

_____

_____

_____

_____

_____

_____

_____

_____

_____

_____

_____

_____

_____

_____

_____

_____

_____

_____

_____

_____

_____

_____

_____

_____

_____

_____

_____

What shall I render unto the LORD for all his benefits toward me?
PSALM 116:12

There is therefore now no condemnation to them
which are in Christ Jesus.
ROMANS 8:1

_____

_____

_____

_____

_____

_____

_____

_____

_____

_____

_____

_____

_____

_____

_____

_____

_____

Blessed are the poor in spirit: for theirs is the kingdom of heaven.
MATTHEW 5:3

God is our refuge and strength, a very present help in trouble.
PSALM 46:1

_____

_____

_____

_____

_____

_____

_____

_____

_____

_____

_____

_____

_____

_____

_____

_____

When Christ, who is our life, shall appear, then shall ye also appear with him in glory.
COLOSSIANS 3:4

O LORD, how great are thy works! and thy thoughts are very deep.
PSALM 92:5

_____

_____

_____

_____

_____

_____

_____

_____

_____

_____

_____

_____

_____

_____

_____

Be of good cheer; I have overcome the world.
JOHN 16:33

Let us come before his presence with thanksgiving, and make a joyful noise unto him with psalms.

PSALM 95:2

_____

_____

_____

_____

_____

_____

_____

_____

_____

_____

_____

_____

_____

_____

_____

_____

Grace to you, and peace, from God our Father and the Lord Jesus Christ.

PHILEMON 3

Fear not, O land; be glad and rejoice:
for the LORD will do great things.
JOEL 2:21

_____

_____

_____

_____

_____

_____

_____

_____

_____

_____

_____

_____

_____

_____

_____

Let this mind be in you, which was also in Christ Jesus.
PHILIPPIANS 2:5

Thou, LORD, hast made me glad through thy work:
I will triumph in the works of thy hands.

PSALM 92:4

_____

_____

_____

_____

_____

_____

_____

_____

_____

_____

_____

_____

_____

_____

_____

Ye are all the children of God by faith in Christ Jesus.
GALATIANS 3:26

And Jesus looking upon them saith, With men it is impossible,
but not with God: for with God all things are possible.

MARK 10:27

_____

_____

_____

_____

_____

_____

_____

_____

_____

_____

_____

_____

_____

_____

_____

_____

_____

_____

_____

_____

_____

_____

_____

_____

_____

_____

_____

_____

_____

_____

_____

*Thou art my hope, O Lord GOD: thou art my trust
from my youth.*
PSALM 71:5

*Herein is love, not that we loved God, but that he loved us, and
sent his Son to be the propitiation for our sins.*

1 JOHN 4:10

_____

_____

_____

_____

_____

_____

_____

_____

_____

_____

_____

_____

_____

_____

I will sing a new song unto thee, O God: upon a psaltery and an instrument of ten strings will I sing praises unto thee.
PSALM 144:9

Being justified by faith, we have peace with God through our Lord Jesus Christ.

ROMANS 5:1

_____

_____

_____

_____

_____

_____

_____

_____

_____

_____

_____

_____

_____

_____

The LORD of hosts is with us; the God of Jacob is our refuge.
PSALM 46:7

*It is God which worketh in you both to will
and to do of his good pleasure.*
PHILIPPIANS 2:13

_By him therefore let us offer the sacrifice of praise to God con-
tinually, that is, the fruit of our lips giving thanks to his name._
HEBREWS 13:15

Comfort ye, comfort ye my people, saith your God.
ISAIAH 40:1

_____

_____

_____

_____

_____

_____

_____

_____

_____

_____

_____

_____

_____

_____

I know whom I have believed, and am persuaded that he is able to keep that which I have committed unto him against that day.
2 TIMOTHY 1:12

They that sow in tears shall reap in joy.
PSALM 126:5

_____

_____

_____

_____

_____

_____

_____

_____

_____

_____

_____

_____

_____

For as many as are led by the Spirit of God,
they are the sons of God.
ROMANS 8:14

Those that be planted in the house of the LORD
shall flourish in the courts of our God.
PSALM 92:13

_____

_____

_____

_____

_____

_____

_____

_____

_____

_____

_____

_____

_____

_____

_____

_____

_____

I press toward the mark for the prize of the high calling of God in Christ Jesus.
PHILIPPIANS 3:14

His Lord said unto him, Well done, thou good and faithful servant: thou hast been faithful over a few things, I will make thee ruler over many things: enter thou into the joy of thy Lord.
MATTHEW 25:21

_____

_____

_____

_____

_____

_____

_____

_____

_____

_____

_____

_____

_____

_____

_____

. . .the living God, who giveth us richly all things to enjoy.
1 TIMOTHY 6:17

They that fear thee will be glad when they see me;
because I have hoped in thy word.
PSALM 119:74

_____

_____

_____

_____

_____

_____

_____

_____

_____

_____

_____

_____

_____

_____

_____

I beseech you therefore, brethren, by the mercies of God, that ye present your bodies a living sacrifice, holy, acceptable unto God, which is your reasonable service.

ROMANS 12:1

Rejoice evermore.
1 THESSALONIANS 5:16

_____

_____

_____

_____

_____

_____

_____

_____

_____

_____

_____

_____

_____

_____

Abide in me, and I in you. As the branch cannot bear fruit of itself, except it abide in the vine; no more can ye, except ye abide in me.

JOHN 15:4

In all these things we are more than conquerors through him that loved us.

ROMANS 8:37

_____

_____

_____

_____

_____

_____

_____

_____

_____

_____

_____

_____

_____

_____

_____

_____

_____

_____

_____

_____

The righteous shall flourish like the palm tree:
he shall grow like a cedar in Lebanon.
PSALM 92:12

He that cometh to God must believe that he is, and that he is a
rewarder of them that diligently seek him.
HEBREWS 11:6

Glory and honour are in his presence;
strength and gladness are in his place.
1 CHRONICLES 16:27

O taste and see that the LORD is good:
blessed is the man that trusteth in him.
PSALM 34:8

_____

_____

_____

_____

_____

_____

_____

_____

_____

_____

_____

_____

_____

_____

_____

_____

And if ye be Christ's, then are ye Abraham's seed, and heirs according to the promise.
GALATIANS 3:29

Blessed be the God and Father of our Lord Jesus Christ, which according to his abundant mercy hath begotten us again unto a lively hope by the resurrection of Jesus Christ from the dead.

1 PETER 1:3

_____

_____

_____

_____

_____

_____

_____

_____

_____

_____

_____

_____

_____

_____

_____

_____

Thou hast turned for me my mourning into dancing: thou hast put off my sackcloth, and girded me with gladness.
PSALM 30:11

Worthy is the Lamb that was slain to receive power, and riches, and wisdom, and strength, and honour, and glory, and blessing.

REVELATION 5:12

If God be for us, who can be against us?
ROMANS 8:31

*Know ye that the LORD he is God: it is he that hath
made us, and not we ourselves; we are his people,
and the sheep of his pasture.*
PSALM 100:3

_____

_____

_____

_____

_____

_____

_____

_____

_____

_____

_____

_____

_____

_____

_____

_____

_____

_____

_____

_____

_____

_____

_____

_____

_____

_____

_____

_____

_____

_____

_____

_____

_____

And he said, The things which are impossible with men are possible with God.
LUKE 18:27

For God so loved the world, that he gave his only begotten Son,
that whosoever believeth in him should not perish,
but have everlasting life.
JOHN 3:16

_____

_____

_____

_____

_____

_____

_____

_____

_____

_____

_____

_____

_____

_____

_____

_____

_I will sing unto the LORD as long as I live: I will sing praise to
my God while I have my being._
PSALM 104:33

Follow peace with all men, and holiness, without which no man shall see the Lord.

HEBREWS 12:14

_____

_____

_____

_____

_____

_____

_____

_____

_____

_____

_____

_____

_____

_____

_____

Blessed are the merciful: for they shall obtain mercy.
MATTHEW 5:7

I will love thee, O LORD, my strength.
PSALM 18:1

_____

_____

_____

_____

_____

_____

_____

_____

_____

_____

_____

_____

_____

_____

_____

The fruit of righteousness is sown in peace of them that make peace.
JAMES 3:18

The LORD is my strength and song,
and he is become my salvation.
EXODUS 15:2

_____

_____

_____

_____

_____

_____

_____

_____

_____

_____

_____

_____

_____

_____

They that trust in the LORD shall be as mount Zion,
which cannot be removed, but abideth for ever.
PSALM 125:1

Blessed are they that hear the word of God, and keep it.
LUKE 11:28

_____

_____

_____

_____

_____

_____

_____

_____

_____

_____

_____

_____

_____

_____

_____

_____

_____

_____

_____

_He that spared not his own Son, but delivered him up for us all,
how shall he not with him also freely give us all things?_
ROMANS 8:32

*The LORD is good to all: and his tender mercies
are over all his works.*
PSALM 145:9

_____

_____

_____

_____

_____

_____

_____

_____

_____

_____

_____

_____

_____

_____

And God shall wipe away all tears from their eyes; and there shall be no more death, neither sorrow, nor crying, neither shall there be any more pain.

REVELATION 21:4